A Note to Parents and Teachers

DK READERS is a compelling reading program for children, designed in conjunction with leading literacy experts, including Dr. Linda Gambrell, Professor of Education at Clemson University. Dr. Gambrell has served as President of the National Reading Conference, College Reading Association, and has recently been elected to serve as President of the International Reading Association.

Beautiful illustrations and superb full-color photographs combine with engaging, easy-to-read stories to offer a fresh approach to each subject in the series. Each DK READER is guaranteed to capture a child's interest while developing his or her reading skills, general knowledge, and love of reading.

The five levels of DK READERS are aimed at different reading abilities, enabling you to choose the books that are exactly right for your child:

Pre-level 1 – Learning to read

Level 1 – Beginning to read

Level 2 – Beginning to read alone

Level 3 – Reading alone

Level 4 – Proficient readers

The "normal" age at which a child begins to read can be anywhere from three to eight years old, so these levels are only a general guideline.

No matter which level you select, you can be sure that you are helping your child learn to read, then read to learn!

LONDON, NEW YORK, MUNICH,
MELBOURNE, AND DELHI

Created by Tall Tree Ltd.
Editor Kate Simkins
Designer Ed Simkins

For DK Publishing
Design Manager Rob Perry
Publishing Manager Simon Beecroft
Category Publisher Alex Allan
DTP Designer Lauren Egan
Production Rochelle Talary

For Marvel
Editors Mickey Stern and Carl Suecoff

Reading Consultant
Linda B. Gambrell

First American Edition, 2006
Published in the United States by
DK Publishing, Inc.
375 Hudson Street
New York, New York 10014

06 07 08 10 10 9 8 7 6 5 4 3 2 1

Published in Great Britain by Dorling Kindersley Limited.

A catalog reccord for this book is available from the
Library of Congress.

ISBN-13: 978-0-75662-025-7 (paperback)
ISBN-10: 0-7566-2025-2 (paperback)
ISBN-13: 978-0-75662-026-4 (hardcover)
ISBN 0-7566-2026-0 (hardcover)

Color reproduction by Media Development and Printing, UK
Printed and bound by L. Rex Printing Co. Ltd, China

Discover more at
www.dk.com

DK READERS

SPIDER-MAN
The Amazing Story
Catherine Saunders

BEGINNING **1** TO READ

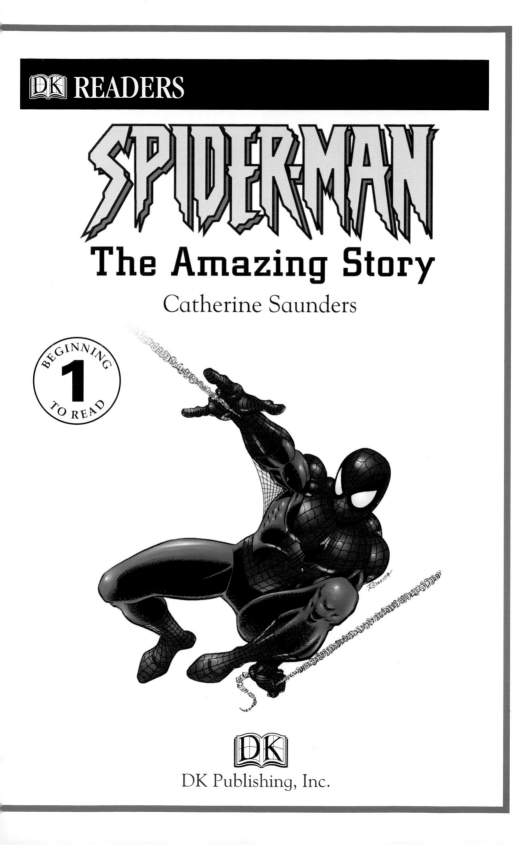

DK
DK Publishing, Inc.

Spider-Man's real name is Peter Parker. Peter was an ordinary boy.

He lived in
New York City with
his Aunt May and
Uncle Ben.
Peter often dreamed
of being a Super Hero.

Spider-Man

Peter Parker was a student at
Midtown High School.
He was very clever and worked
hard at his lessons.

He always got good marks and his favorite subject was science.

student

Peter was a quiet, shy boy who did not have many friends.

He was not very good at sports, and he was afraid of heights.

Other students, like Flash Thompson, sometimes made fun of him.

One day, Peter Parker's life changed forever.
He was bitten by a radioactive spider at a science exhibition.

The spider's poison entered
Peter's body and
made him start to change.
He felt very strange!

spider

The spider's bite gave
Peter fantastic new powers.

He became
really strong
and could climb
tall skyscrapers.

skyscrapers

Peter decided to become
a wrestling star on television.
He called himself Spider-Man.

One day, Uncle Ben was killed by a burglar.
This made Peter decide to use his amazing powers to help people and catch criminals.

BEN PARKER

HE WAS LOVED

burglar

Peter turned Spider-Man
from a television star into
a Super Hero!

Spider-Man's special costume and mask protect his true identity from his enemies.

costume

Peter wears his Spider-Man
costume under his clothes.
He is always ready to leap
into action!

Every spider has a web.
Peter Parker used the science
he learned in school
to make Spider-Man's web.

Spider-Man shoots the web
from his wrists.
   He uses it to swing
      from building to building.

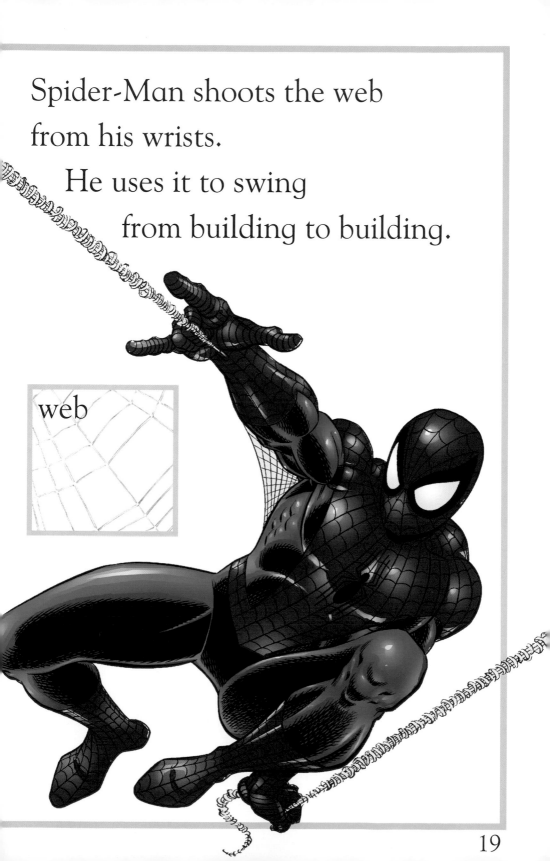

web

Spider-Man is always one step
ahead of danger, thanks to
his spider-sense.

He can tell if any of his enemies
are trying to sneak up on him.
His spider-sense even works
in the dark.

Spider-Man has
amazing strength.
He can bend iron bars and
punch through walls.

rooftops

He can also jump higher
than a house and
leap across the rooftops.

Spider-Man can also think
very quickly.
This makes him good at catching
even the cleverest criminals.

Spider-Man has many enemies,
like the Scorpion and
Doctor Octopus.

Peter Parker is in love with
Mary Jane Watson,
who lives
next door.

Mary Jane likes Peter.
She secretly thinks that
he might be Spider-Man.

Spider-Man usually works alone,
but sometimes even he needs help
from his Super Hero friends.

Daredevil and Captain America
have both helped Spider-Man
to fight crime.

Peter Parker knows that
his powers make him different
from other people.
He believes that Spider-Man must
help people who need him.

Spider-Man does his best
to make the world a safer place.

Picture word list

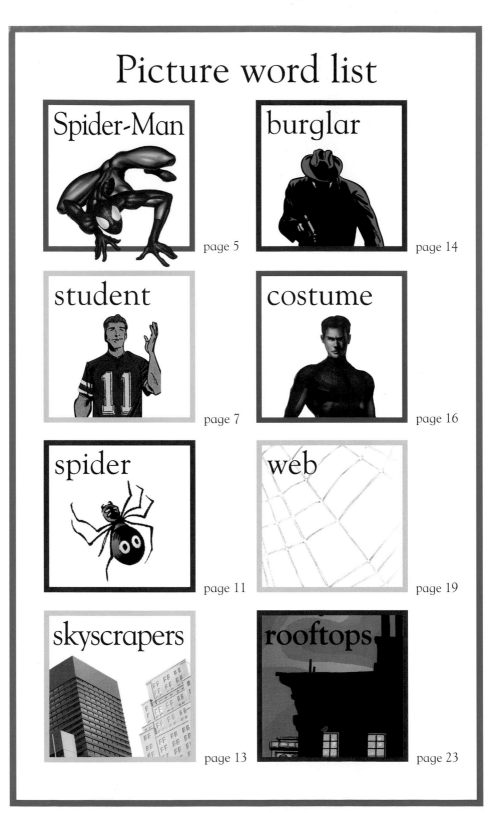

Spider-Man
page 5

burglar
page 14

student
page 7

costume
page 16

spider
page 11

web
page 19

skyscrapers
page 13

rooftops
page 23